The Early Tozer:
A Word in Season

The EARLY TOZER:
A WORD in SEASON

SELECTED ARTICLES AND QUOTATIONS

Compiled by
JAMES L. SNYDER

✝ Christian Publications
CAMP HILL, PENNSYLVANIA

Christian Publications
3825 Hartzdale Drive
Camp Hill, PA 17011

Faithful, biblical publishing since 1883

ISBN: 0-87509-710-3
LOC Catalog Card Number: 97-65120

Table of Contents

Preface

In the 1930s and '40s A.W. Tozer wrote a regular column for *The Alliance Weekly*, now *Alliance Life*. The selected columns published here were written prior to the publication of *The Pursuit of God* and widely accepted among Christians at the time. It was these writings that led to Tozer's eventual election as editor of *The Alliance Weekly* (1950-1963), from which he gained international acclaim as a writer with keen spiritual perception and as a rising star in the world of evangelical literature.

In these short essays Tozer hones the craft by which he would later become famous. Here you will find wit, humor, spiritual insight and the discriminating observations of a man of God.

These are not sermons. He does not have the pulpit in mind. They are not articles in the truest sense of the word; rather they are the casual musings of a man in tune with not only the world around him, but with God. They have the feel of the common person. Tozer has in mind the truck driver, the New York cabby, the housewife "up the hollow." These are not theological treatises, although they deal with great theological issues. You will smile at Tozer's admonition: "Let's keep the Bible in the pulpit, and as far as possible keep the donkeys out!"

Tozer wrote many of these essays while riding the train to the numerous speaking engagements he had in those days. He was always writing, always thinking and trying to put into words the thoughts dancing in his head. He was worshiping. God was breathing into his soul the essence of what it means to be a Christian, and Tozer responded by writing. Always writing. Always putting those thoughts into prose.

When comparing these early columns to his later writings, one can see that Tozer's style improved remarkably over the years. Interestingly enough, the message did not change too much. For the pilgrim en route to the Celestial City, these essays of the early Tozer are truly "a word in season."

James L. Snyder
February 16, 1996
Ocala, Florida

1

The Four Classes
of Bible Characters

Bible characters fall into four classes: those who are great but not good; those who are good but not great; those who are neither good nor great; and those who are both great and good.

Among those who are great but not good are Joab, Nebuchadnezzar, Sennacherib. Of the good who are not great we may name Isaac, Elkanah and Joseph the husband of Mary. Neither great nor good are Eli, Shimei, Ahab. Of those who are both good and great, the most famous would be Abraham, Moses, David and Paul. A few speckled souls, as Balaam, Samson and Solomon, may need a fifth class to accommodate them. Their checkered characters make classification difficult.

Under these heads may be arranged not only all Bible characters, but the whole world and all of history. Each one of us is in one or another of these classes. A mighty lot depends upon which one.

Goodness is possible to all, greatness to a few. Salvation makes a man good but not necessarily great. Greatness contributes nothing to any man's happiness; goodness, everything; yet all men desire to be great, and only a few desire to be good. Greatness requires a combination of qualities rare in nature; goodness is a gift of God and may be acquired by the humblest of men. Greatness will count for nothing in the day of judgment; goodness will be rewarded before the eyes of all.

We have made a disastrous mistake in holding up our great men as models to youth; good men should rather serve for their examples.

A great man may be miserable in this world and wretched in the world to come; a truly good man will not be miserable for long even in this world, and in the future world he will be comforted in the bosom of Abraham.

2

We Are in Debt to God

WE ARE all in debt to the universe; we have
nothing we did not receive. To our parents
we owe our very existence; to leaders, pioneers,
inventors, we owe every comfort we possess above
the average. To our political fathers we in America owe our freedom. To the brave men who have
died in all our wars we owe the blessing of a free
and prosperous country.

To the gifted great of the past we owe every
lovely picture, every sweet song, every notable
book. Around us we see little or nothing for which
we can properly claim credit. Labor-saving de-
vices, our excellent school system, highways,
parks and museums all are the work of other
hearts and other hands. We are the heirs of the
ages; we reap where we have not sown and gather
where we have not planted.

All good and beneficial things the world affords
are gifts of Almighty God and come to us out of
His lovingkindness. Add to these all the wealth of

grace which comes to us through blood atonement: revelation, redemption, mercy, the gift of eternal life and the indwelling Spirit. For all this, for everything, we are in debt to God forever. We can never repay our heavenly Father for the least of His goodness.

In view of all these things, a thankless man must be a bad man if for no other reason than that he is thankless. Ingratitude is a major sin. The man of enlightened mind will always feel deeply humbled when he considers God's goodness and his own insignificance. He is likely to be very modest about demanding anything further; he will be too conscious that he already enjoys far more than the circumstances warrant.

3

God Requires Sincerity

WE LIVE like civilized men, but we go back six thousand years to do our dying. The curse of artificiality which infects our modern life disappears for a moment when we are born and forever when we die. Birth and death remain untouched by the hand of change. We see life in the raw at its beginning and at its close.

In the depths of our universal beings we remain essentially primitive; our culture affects little more than the surface.

There are numberless distinctions between men involving acquired habits, tastes, modes of speech; but when the heart is moved deeply enough, these distinctions disappear. Who can tell as he listens to the cry of a bereaved mother whether she comes from the avenue or from the slums? We speak like educated persons, but we weep like primitive men.

The heart has a universal language known to all men. It is this language which Christ speaks. He directs His call to the ancient human heart of mankind. For this reason His message needs little modification for different classes of hearers. That which differentiates is incidental. Christ searches for the essential man beneath his disguises, and as the Son of Man He is instantly understood.

This adds up to one thing: Be absolutely sincere in every dealing with God. Veneer, pose, efforts to impress—all are offensive to Him. We must put away all pretense and come to Him in our true characters as fallen sons and daughters of Adam and Eve. It is such the Lord came to seek and to save.

4

Check with God First

To get to the truth I recommend a plain text Bible and the diligent application of two knees to the floor. Beware of too many footnotes. The rabbis of Israel took to appending notes to the inspired text, with the result that a great body of doctrine grew up which finally crowded out the Scriptures themselves. This mass of interpretation was called the Talmud and was for generations taught as the very truth of God. Jesus referred to this when He said, "Howbeit in vain do they worship me, teaching for doctrines the commandments of men" (Mark 7:7).

It is a dangerous and costly practice to consult men every time we reach a dark spot in the Scriptures. We do not overlook the importance of the gift of teaching to the Church, but we do warn against the habit of taking by blind faith the opinions of men—even good men. A few minutes of earnest prayer will often give more light than hours of reading the commentaries.

And the commentators—how disappointing they are! Up to now I cannot recall a single instance where they have given me light on the point that bothered me. They usually wax eloquent on the things we all know and pass over in silence the verses "hard to be understood." In so doing they merely bear witness to their own humanity. No one knows too much, even as you and I.

An expensive cover and a complicated index will often awe the young seeker into a state of mental passivity where he would never dare to disagree with what he reads on those sacred pages. There is something about the smell of a well-bound book that is hard to resist! Well, reading another commentator will serve as a corrective against a too-great credulity, for they frequently disagree with each other. The shock produced by an irresistible force meeting an immovable body is small compared with that experienced by a young Christian who for the first time finds two "infallible" teachers contradicting each other. But if the fledgling saint can survive the shock he will be better off, for he will be driven to trust the Holy Spirit for light, and that is worth almost any price.

The best rule is: Go to God first about the meaning of any text. Then consult the teachers. They may have found a grain of wheat you had overlooked.

5

The Puttering Pastor

CHRISTIAN MINISTRY is conceded to be the noblest of professions. It is also attended with greatest dangers.

The ministry affords limitless opportunity for the lazy man to indulge his talents. Doing nothing can be accomplished more gracefully in the Lord's work than anywhere else for the simple reason that the minister has no one to check up on him. The average church requires little of its pastor except to mark time decorously; the preacher with a propensity for loafing is strongly tempted to do just that.

Many a minister who would be shocked at the thought of doing nothing nevertheless gets nothing done because he has acquired the habit of frittering away his time. Late hours, requiring compensatory late sleeping, several trips to the store, assisting with the family laundry, standing in line to buy a reservation for his wife's niece who is going on a visit to Keokuk—these things, or others like them, eat up the time and leave him spent and empty at the end of the day.

After a day occupied with trifles, our prophet faces his audience in the evening mentally and spiritually out of tune and altogether unprepared for the holy task before him. His confused smile is attributed to his humility. The audience is tolerant. They know that he has nothing worthwhile to say, but they figure that he has been so busy with his pastoral duties he has not had time to study. They generously forgive him and accept his threadbare offering as the best they can expect under the circumstances.

However much we may dislike to hear it, loafing and puttering are deadly habits for the young minister. He will either conquer them or they will break him.

6

The Value of Good Habits

A HABIT is a useful servant, but a dangerous master.

The better the habit the greater the danger.

Bad habits disturb the conscience and create a sense of inward uneasiness. Often a sudden shock, the sight of death, a good gospel sermon, the quiet rebuke of a friend will throw the man of evil habit into a state of mental anguish. Isaiah had it right when he said, "The wicked are like the troubled sea, when it cannot rest, whose waters cast up mire and dirt" (Isaiah 57:20).

Good habits may, on the contrary, unless great care is taken, put the heart into a smiling sleep. "As far as that matter is concerned," says the conscience, "I need trouble myself no more about it. It is taken care of." Thus the life loses its spontaneity and becomes conventionalized. The good act is continued after the reason for it has gone from the life. The result is a perfunctory and wooden Christianity.

Religious habits can deceive the possessor as few things can do. As far as I know, a habit and a mud turtle are the only things in nature that can walk around after they are dead. For instance, many a man has returned thanks at the table faithfully for many years and yet has never once really prayed from the heart during all that time. The life died out of the habit long ago, but the habit itself persisted in the form of a meaningless mumble.

The point is that we should put away every useless habit, reject all patented religious phrases, refuse to follow other people's visions. We should insist upon living wholly from within. This encourages a childlike simplicity in life, very pleasing to God, and a source of great strength to the soul.

7

God Evaluates Our Average

To GET quick and easy results at the altar the evangelist will sometimes resort to a little gem of specious logic cast in some such language as this: "If you have ever enjoyed a better moment than you are enjoying right now, then you are backslidden, and you should come forward at once and get right with God."

That net is practically sucker-proof; nothing will slip through but the polliwogs.

Look at the record: Moses was forty days and forty nights on the mount in intimate communion with God; after that he came down to a lower plane and spent forty years walking by faith in obedience to the Lord's instructions. Isaiah had one mighty revolutionizing vision of God high and lifted up, but as far as we know he never had another. Paul was caught up once into the third heaven; from then on he had to be content to walk the earth like any other man.

In baseball a man will sometimes "play over his

own head," which is to say that he will, for a brief time, rise above his average ability as a day-by-day player. No manager would sign a man on such an erratic performance. He wants to know what the player is capable of doing game after game against all kinds of opposition.

A man's true character is the average of his life, not the extremes. David reached the top when he slew Goliath and the bottom when he slew Uriah. In one instance he went above his average, in the other he went below it. The real David is found between the two.

We should not be too much elated over a victory nor too much discouraged over a defeat. God reckons the average and will evaluate us accordingly.

8

The State of Ancient Saints

I<small>T IS</small> disappointing that there are so few sweet old saints among us. The nature of the gospel is such as to encourage us to expect the children of God to grow tender and more Christlike as the years go on. Old age should find us like the woods in autumn, lovely with the varied pastels of the Spirit. Too often it finds us bitter, intolerant and a sore trial to those who have to live with us.

There are few sadder sights than that of an old man who has outlived his generation and his usefulness, but who, for some reason, still lingers on, staring with crusty disfavor at any servant of the Lord, however humble, who may be for the moment in a place of prominence in the kingdom of God.

The knowledge that he is no longer needed is like gall and wormwood to the soul of such a man. All who once appreciated him are gone. He is filled with sour resentment that the work of the Lord can manage to muddle along without him, and he takes arbitrary revenge by discounting every effort made by anyone now living.

Like a robin in the snow he stands silent as the chill of his own spirit. When he does open his mouth it is to chirp a querulous and reminiscent elegy to a glory that has departed from the earth. He is fully convinced that the grave has reaped a total harvest of righteousness (his lone self excepted) and that no man now on earth can be big or honest or sincere. If there were any such they would be dead; anyone should be able to see that!

Lot's wife looked back and was turned to salt; there is danger that we look back and be turned to acid.

9

Jesus Christ Is Every Man's Contemporary

JESUS CHRIST is every man's contemporary. With Him there is nothing new and nothing old, no one modern and no one old-fashioned.

To praise the past and cry down the present is to localize Christ in time and strip Him of some of the very qualities which enabled Him to be the Savior of the world.

There is no need to speak of "the time of Christ" nor to sing plaintively, "I should like to have been with Him then." This is the time of Christ. Today is as near to Him as yesterday. It is as near to Him from the twentieth century as from the first, from North America as from Jerusalem.

Jesus stands at the center of the world's life. He is (if we may borrow a figure) the Hub of the wheel; everyone and everything are on the rim, equally near to Him and equally distant from Him.

Christ is not only the Son of Abraham, He is the Son of Adam and the Son of man. So He is every man's countryman, at home anywhere. H.G. Wells has given it as his opinion that Buddhism is the best of the world's great religions. He admits, however, that it can flourish in no countries except those having a warm climate! Christianity knows no such limitations. Christ stands above and outside of race and time, of climate and social customs.

Salvation is an internal thing and is wholly independent of externals. Any man who will admit Christ into his heart will recognize Him instantly as a Brother.

10

The Necessity of Honoring God

THE GLORY of God is the health of the universe; the essential soundness of things requires that He be honored among created intelligences.

Where God is honored fully is heaven, and it is heaven for that reason; where He is honored not at all is hell, and for that cause it is hell. Among men we see a mixture of honor and dishonor. Basically this is the cause back of earth's tragic, confused history.

God has not finished with His saints till He has brought them to a place where they honor Him on earth as He is honored in heaven.

God gives away His full purpose in redeeming man when He says, "Thou art my servant, O Israel, in whom I will be glorified" (Isaiah 49:3).

If we can convince God that we are sold out to His high honor, the problem of unanswered prayer is solved. God will withhold nothing from that man who is determined to live to His glory alone.

The sinful instinct to arrogate to ourselves some

19

amount at least of praise is deep-seated and hard to destroy.

But there is hope for us nevertheless.

At the cross human pride withers like the cursed fig tree, from the root up. There will be a period of agonized struggle when life-loving old Adam is led out to die; but if the Christian will have the courage to go through with it, the whole quality of his life will be changed from that moment on.

God has said, "them that honour me I will honour" (1 Samuel 2:30). He can honor us only when He knows His glory is safe in our hands.

11

The Danger of Judging Others

THE DEEPEST of all deep things is the human heart. No man can fully know his own, and it follows that no man can ever know the heart of another.

For this reason it is dangerous to judge any Christian's conduct or character. There is too great a likelihood that we will misjudge from plain lack of knowledge of our subject.

The Christian public has been amazingly kind to me. I have not one fault to find with the treatment accorded me by my longsuffering brethren. But when I have sometimes run afoul of the critics it has been my experience to have them fasten on some trifling fault that did not matter, as the old writers would say, "a farthing," and blindly pass over the really serious ones without noticing them.

I have on a few occasions been toasted a rich brown over some personal idiosyncrasy which could not possibly do any harm, while the big weaknesses that really give me trouble were either ignored altogether or made to pass for virtues.

"Judge not, that ye be not judged" (Matthew 7:1) is still a mighty safe rule to follow. The Christian who will be always panning others will surely come in for a session on the hot griddle himself sooner or later. And he won't get much help from the Lord when the time comes. He asked for it.

12

The Cross Did Not Change God

THE CROSS did not change God. "I am the LORD, I change not" (Malachi 3:6).

The work of Christ on the cross did not influence God to love us, did not increase that love by one degree, did not open any fount of grace or mercy in His heart. He had loved us from old eternity and needed nothing to stimulate that love. The cross is not responsible for God's love; rather it was His love which conceived the cross as the one method by which we could be saved.

God felt no different toward us after Christ had died for us, for in the mind of God Christ had already died before the foundation of the world. God never saw us except through atonement. The human race could not have existed one day in its fallen state had not Christ spread His mantle of atonement over it. And this He did in eternal purpose long ages before they led Him out to die on the hill above Jerusalem. All God's dealings with man have been conditioned upon the cross.

Much unworthy thinking has been done about the cross, and a lot of injurious teaching has resulted. The idea that Christ rushed in breathless to catch the upraised arm of God ready to descend in fury upon us is not drawn from the Bible. It has arisen from the necessary limitations of human speech in attempting to set forth the fathomless mystery of atonement.

Neither is the picture of Christ, going out trembling to the cross to appease the wrath of God, in accordance with the truth. The Scriptures never represent the Persons of the Trinity as opposed to or in disagreement with each other. The Holy Three have ever been and will forever be one in essence, in love, in purpose.

We have been redeemed not by one Person of the Trinity putting Himself against another, but by the three Persons working in the ancient and glorious harmony of the Godhead.

13

God Blesses Us on His Terms

GOD'S LOVE makes His blessings available to all without money and without price. Grace operates in a sphere where human merit cannot enter. "For by grace are ye saved through faith; and that not of yourselves: it is the gift of God" (Ephesians 2:8).

We must not, however, overlook the fact that God's benefits are dispensed according to promise, and that each promise carries with it specific conditions which must be met if it is to be honored. Every blessing has its own terms; meet them and the blessing is yours.

Our chief difficulty in dealing with God is the habit of trying to make our own terms instead of meeting the terms already laid down. With our mouths we sturdily deny that weeping has any value, but I fear that in our hearts we are often guilty of embracing the heresy of tears. We sometimes allow our natural sympathy to throw us over on the side of rebellious humanity against God Himself.

That there are holy tears no one will deny, but who has not seen at an altar the vexed weeping of stubborn souls angry with God for refusing to yield His sovereignty to their importunate demands?

It would be well for us if we could learn early the futility of trying to obtain forbidden things by overpersuading God. He will not be thus stampeded. Anything that falls within the circle of His will He gives freely to whosoever asks aright, but not days or weeks of fasting and prayer will persuade Him to alter anything that has gone out of His mouth.

In fairness to the whole truth we should recall two apparent exceptions to this rule. God did bend His will to give Israel flesh in the wilderness, and He did, against His own desires, give them a king. But for these two breaches Israel had to pay in tears and blood.

That is a price too high to consider.

If we would but quickly surrender to the will of God we could the sooner begin to enjoy His blessings.

If our love were but more simple
We should take Him at His word:
And our lives would be all sunshine
In the sweetness of our Lord.

14

On Concentrated Vis

O NE TROUBLE with us today is that we know too many things.

The whole trend of the moment is toward the accumulation of a multitude of unrelated facts without a unifying philosophy to give them meaning.

The neat little digest magazines tend to encourage faith in the idea-hopping type of study. This produces an informed superficiality worse in many ways than ignorance itself.

The ironical comment made on a certain scholar seems pertinent, "He is studying Greek now. Soon he will know a little Greek——then he will know a little everything."

A few great ideas are better than a score of unimportant ones. Lincoln rose to earthly immortality on no more than two major ideas held with all the power of his soul. They were: "Slavery must be destroyed. The Union must he preserved." While the little politicians cavilled over trifles, he

vision the two things that mattered
time. Those two things made Lincoln.

The ability to recognize the few ideas that
count and the determination to stay by them have
always been marks of greatness. Daniel purposed
in his heart; Paul said, "This one thing I do"
(Philippians 3:13); Moody heard a voice say, "Save
all you can." Simpson cried of the heathen, "We
must go and tell them."

Those single ideas drove these men like engines
within their souls. Though fully capable of enter-
taining unlimited number of ideas, they were wise
enough to hit upon the few that mattered and
work them without ceasing.

The prophets and reformers of the past were
men of few but mighty convictions. Their very
narrowness secured high compression and gave
added power to their lives.

Hesitation and indecision mark too many religious leaders of our day. This results directly
from lack of conviction. These prophets have seen
so many visions they are unable to tell which one
is from God. They hear so many voices they are
never able to say with certainty, "Thus saith the
Lord."

15

Lay the Proper Stress

I N EVERY sentence there are the strong structural words, the nouns and verbs, without which the sentence would have no meaning at all; and there are in addition certain weak words, the connectives and modifiers, which could be omitted without too much loss to the total meaning.

The verbs and nouns denote being, action, persons, things and are thus of major importance; the other words denote differences, directions, relationships and are of minor importance only.

In every paragraph the good reader will know where to lay his stress; he will sense the major words and lay the weight there. To stress the unimportant words is to invert the meaning; to stress every word alike is to cancel all meaning entirely.

In the Christian's total creed also there are the majors and the minors, and these must be carefully distinguished if his faith is to have symmetry. Some tenets hold positions of key importance vitally necessary to the whole structure: the existence of God, the divine inspiration of the Scriptures, the deity of Christ, the efficacy of atonement; these, with a few others, are the majors. But the minors are there also: modes of baptism, church polity, frequency and manner of observing the Lord's Supper; such as these are the minors and should be recognized as such and never given an emphasis that will destroy the harmony of the whole; and especially should they never be allowed to disturb the unity of the brotherhood of Christian believers.

Many a splendid church has drifted into modernism because its leaders would not insist on the everlasting importance of the basic doctrines of the faith; and many a church split has resulted from an undue attachment to nonessentials.

Contending for the faith once delivered to the saints may not always mean fighting to retain the major tenets of the Christian creed. It can mean, as well, striving to maintain a proper balance between all the doctrines of the faith in their relation to each other and to the whole.

Overstress the minors, and you have chaos; overlook the majors, and you have death.

16

Our Hope Is in Our Changeablilty

"ALL THINGS are become new." Paul here in Second Corinthians 5:17 describes a change in the life as complete as it is possible to experience and still permit the individual to remain the same entity. To make the change any more radical it would be necessary for God to blot the man out and start over.

Every hope for the human race is based upon the assumption that the nature of man can be changed from what it is to what it ought to be. Were the character of the individual static, all hope for the world would perish instantly.

While human nature is in its present fairly fluid condition, it can be altered. The whole method of God in salvation proceeds on the assumption that men can be changed. Their present evil state need not be final.

Salvation achieves a fundamental change in

the spiritual essence of the saved one and accomplishes a transformation of inward tendencies so complete as to secure a flat reversal of direction in the flow of external conduct.

It is thought by many that before a man is saved there is first a secret work of God carried on within his soul, a kind of sovereign breathing upon the dry bones in preparation for the mighty change which is to follow. However that may be, the first point at which any work of God breaks through to our consciousness is in conviction, and the first place where it becomes morally effective is in repentance.

For be it remembered: Repentance is a moral change. It is in essence a thorough alteration of the life, a full changeover from one kind of living to another, and it embraces the whole man outside and in.

Few worse calamities could be imagined for us than to have our lives "frozen" at their present levels. That we are not now finished products but rather in the process of spiritual development should be reason for constant rejoicing.

"But we all, with open face beholding as in a glass the glory of the Lord, are changed into the same image from glory to glory, even as by the Spirit of the Lord" (2 Corinthians 3:18).

17

Rooting Out Superstition in Modern Christianity

THE HABIT of attributing to the physical moral or spiritual qualities is deep-rooted and all but impossible to eradicate.

It probably dates back in our racial psychology to a long line of pagan ancestors who were, apparently, willing to worship anything they found lying around loose and who insisted upon finding religious meaning in everything they could not understand.

Any chance object might be holy to them if they suspected that it had a god tucked away in it somewhere, and they considered those places especially holy where some high-ranking deity dwelt, so they had holy trees, holy topographical bumps and holy lean-tos of various sorts in which or toward which they bowed with solemn reverence at certain stated times and seasons.

A good honest look around us will compel the

admission that there is more than a small trace of this superstition left in modern Christian worship as practiced in our churches today.

The New Testament puts all true worship in the Spirit and exposes the complete meaninglessness of mere externalities. "But the hour cometh, and now is, when the true worshippers shall worship the Father in spirit and in truth" (John 4:23).

With these words Christ freed His followers forever from bondage to shrines, "holy" places and religious gadgets of every description. With these we simply have nothing to do. They cannot add one atom to the total glory of true worship nor can the absence of them take anything away.

Am I mistaken, or have I noticed among our churches a drift toward the observation of holy days and new moons and seasons? If such a thing is true, let us revolt against it. Let us throw off the yoke of bondage from which we were, at such great cost, set free.

Every place is a holy place where the foot of the true Christian treads; every Friday is a good Friday to the man of faith and every Sunday Easter. Amen.

18

Jesus Christ and the Common People

T HE SHARP divergence of viewpoint between the Man Christ Jesus and many of His present-day representatives is glaringly seen by comparing His evaluation of the common people with theirs.

Christ did not teach the flat equality of all men. He knew well that some were superior to others and was quick to acknowledge excellence where it might be found. He, however, did not make excellence to consist of talents, neither of social or financial standing. He scorned all differences between men which rested upon mere titles or earthly position. His is an aristocracy of the spirit, and men are rated according to their faith and faithfulness only. He is greatest in the kingdom of God who has best kept the Lord's commandments.

The pitiful eagerness of some of our churches to cultivate men of wealth and influence is in sad contrast to our Lord's utter contempt for the would-be great and His tender solicitude for the plain people. The two attitudes cannot be reconciled. They are not two phases of the same thing: they are two things wholly different from each other. One is of the earth, earthy, and derives from the fallen heart of man; the other belongs to the new creation and flows out of the heart of Christ Himself.

We would do well to seek a new appreciation of the inarticulate many who make up the Body of the Church. They do a large share of the praying and pay most of the bills. Without them not a preacher could carry on, not a Bible school function. They are the flesh and sinews of the missionary program. They are the private soldiers of the Lord who do most of the fighting and get fewest decorations. The big stars of the Church get a lot of their glory now; the plain Christians must wait till the Lord returns. There will be some surprises then.

Our Lord was never very popular with the mighty. After that first experience in the Temple He seems to have had enough of the doctors. He stayed pretty close to the plain people from then on.

If you can't find the Lord among the mighty, look for Him among the lowly: you will find Him there.

19

The Hollywood Mentality

PERHAPS I am growing conservative now that I am well past that time when life is said to begin, but whatever the reason, I confess myself very much distressed over the persistence among religious people of that condition which, for lack of a name, I shall call the Hollywood mentality.

I had been naive enough to believe that we had been disillusioned by the sorry performances of the personality boys of a few years ago and that we had recovered from that form of abnormal psychology which we caught from the movies; but evidently I was too optimistic. Like malaria it's back on us again.

How does the disease work? It distorts the vision so that the victim cannot discern true values in the work of the Lord. He shrugs off impatiently the time-honored ways of the saints and goes out for color, flash, size, vim and zip. Quiet trust, stability, repose—these are passed up in a flurry of religious excitement.

Numbers come first, so anything will do if it will bring a crowd. The most dismal example to come to my notice of the shoddy means used to coax in a crowd appeared on the church page of a big city daily recently: "7:30 p.m., Moving Pictures of Cannibalism." And they were advertising a missionary convention!

The fevered prophets who promote this highly nervous variant of true Christianity long for publicity as a fever patient thirsts for water. It is their life. Their shameless clamor after press notice is evidence enough of their lush carnality, and nobody knows it better than the sarcastic newsmen who have to handle the copy.

Even in some of the best spiritual circles where symptoms are less marked, there is still too much evidence of this disease. Pulpit committees demand big names for their services, and when they are forced sometimes to put up with a humble and obscure servant of the Lord, they sit disappointed and uncomfortable, wondering nervously what the public will think of their man.

Compared with the spirit and teaching of the New Testament, this whole attitude is seen to be unbelieving and earthly, and the results can only be tragic at last.

20

The True Profit
of Bible Reading

BIBLE READING, if it is to be profitable, will not be the pleasant diversion sometimes pictured in the religious ads, a peaceful pastime with which to while away a tired evening.

The Bible is a serious book, probably the most serious in the world, and it will not submit to being used for light amusement. The message of the Bible is strongly evangelistic, its tone is urgent, its claims are exacting. It makes sovereign demands upon the reader and will hear no excuse for his failure to meet them.

The first work of revealed truth is to secure an unconditional surrender of the sinner to the will of God. Until this has been accomplished, nothing really lasting has been done at all. The reader may admire the rich imagery of the Bible, its bold figures and impassioned flights of eloquence; he may enjoy its tender musical passages and revel in its strong homely wisdom; but until he has submitted to its full authority over his life, he has secured no good from it yet.

There is some danger that we degrade the Scriptures into a fetish and unconsciously assume that there is some virtue in the mere reading of them. Without doubt the Word of God should be read more than it is; every Christian should be able to say, "In thy law do I meditate day and night." But it should never be considered an end in itself. No one should be weak enough to take comfort from the fact that he has read his daily portion.

The express purpose of revealed truth is to change people radically and permanently, making them over in the likeness and image of Christ. The Word of God, if it is to achieve this purpose, must receive from the hearer not only belief but active obedience. Without corresponding moral action, a creed may be a snare, and theology a delusion.

It is no credit to a man to have studied the Bible half a century if he cannot discover in himself (and more particularly, if others cannot discover in him) a family resemblance to the Holy Trinity.

We should read the Word in meekness, humility, full trust and ready obedience. Then, and only then, can we know the true profit of Bible reading.

21

The Warm Hearts and Cool Heads of Christians

THE WARMEST hearts and the coolest heads anywhere at any time should always belong to the Christians.

There are sound reasons for this.

The Christian is seated "above." His fortunes do not depend upon earthly circumstances, but upon Christ who has conquered everything and "is set on the right hand of the throne of the Majesty in the heavens" (Hebrews 8:1).

For the warmth of his heart the Christian has the love of God which is "shed abroad" by the Holy Ghost, while from his vantage point in the "heavenly places" he is able to look down calmly upon the excited happenings of men. In his flesh he may be a part of the human scene, but in his spirit he is far above it all and is never at any time too much moved by what he sees.

From the Word of God he learns the direction

things are going and is thus able in God to see the end from the beginning and call the things that are not as though they were.

The life of the Christian is bound up in the sovereignty of God, i.e., His complete freedom in His universe, His full ability to carry out His plans to their triumphant conclusion. Since he is a part of God's eternal purpose, he knows he must win at last, and he can afford to be calm even when the battle seems to be temporarily going against him.

The world has no such "blissful center" upon which to rest and is therefore constantly shifting about, greatly elated today, terribly cast down tomorrow and wildly excited the next day.

The danger is that the Christian, surrounded as he is by the world, may allow himself to be affected by its moods. Right now we must guard ourselves against mass hysteria, war-hysteria, as the tempo and fury of the great war moves upward toward Armageddon intensity, and the hysteria of peace when peace returns again to the blood-slaked and staggering world.

22

The Making of a Superior Christian

W HEN GOD sets out really to make a superior Christian, He is compelled to strip the man of everything that might serve as a false refuge, a secondary trust. He must shut the man up to Himself only or He must give him up to be a second-rate saint.

There is no middle ground.

It is usually no great task to disengage the favored one from the grosser trusts, the more repulsive idols; but there are many innocent trusts as harmful in their effects, deliverance from which is always difficult and may actually prove impossible.

Among these we would name sweet and enjoyable friendships.

It is an experience paralleling physical death to stand alone, bereaved of a friend who had become a living part of the whole emotional life, as necessary, so we feel, as our human heart, as dear as our blood. One of the most pain-filled cries to escape from the soul of the Man of Sorrows was caused by the treachery of one whom He called "mine own familiar friend, in whom I trusted" (Psalm 41:9).

It is easier to lose such a friend in death than to lose him in life. David's grief over his slain friend, Jonathan, had about it some measure of poetic compensation; the loss was a "sweet sorrow," greatly ameliorated by the knowledge that the heart of Jonathan, so cold now and still, belonged to David in death as it had in life. Such sorrow can be borne; but to search into the face of a former friend and see on the dear and familiar features only dark hostility, to feel that the tender heart of one-time affection has been snatched coldly away and is ours no more—this is more painful than death: who can bear it?

God allows such experiences because He would have us all for Himself with no rival to share our hearts or to divide our love. He tears away the vine from the crumbling wall of earthly friendships that He may teach it to cling to the Rock of Ages.

When the full sad work is finished and the heart delivered from its sweet idolatry, He may give the friend back to us again, purified now and harmless. God is good.

23

Maintaining Correct Perspective

THERE ARE two illusions against which we Christians must guard: one is of distance and the other of too close proximity.

The human eye is focused to see properly only within a certain varying distance from itself. When the object is too close or too far away, the eye is confused and fails to report accurately what is before it.

One of the greatest hindrances to spiritual poise and balanced living is the tendency to accept as correct images seen out of focus. What looks to a tired eye like a strange monster walking across the brow of a distant hill may be in reality only a beetle walking across the windowpane close at hand (as every reader of Poe will remember).

If ever we needed to maintain correct perspective, it is now. This mad battle of the giants which is raging with such frightful destructiveness over the face of the world, like Milton's fallen angels, uprooting mountains in its fury, is too close to us for correct appraisal now. We are like men in a small summer cottage with a mighty storm raging about us. The very landscape appears to be enraged; our senses stagger before the wild terror of the world and nature gone mad.

Soon—how soon I do not claim to know, but it will be but a moment in the long sweep of the age—this war will end, and peace will come again. Then the blood-sick and weary nations will set about the job of reconstruction, once more to try to build peace into the structure of the world.

In the meantime we Christians must stand back in spirit from the spinning maelstrom. We must refuse to be panic-stricken by the sound and the fury. We must keep our heads and our faith; the world will need us when this war is over.

We cannot escape the responsibilities our life in the world entails, but we can escape the false philosophy by which the world appraises such times as these. We can insist upon seeing things with the eyes of God; we can let the light of the Word in upon these scenes of terror; we can take the long view and be at rest in our spirits.

24

How to Find Peace in Confusion

WHEN DAVID prayed that he might never be put to confusion, he may have had in mind only some disturbing situation which for the moment distressed him. But the implications are broad and deep.

Confusion is Adam's word. It came in by sin and is a violation of the laws of the mind as originally given by the Creator.

Our minds require order, our passions create confusion. Order is as necessary to peace of heart as is harmony to music. Without it there can be only raucous discord and confusion.

No word could better describe the state of a sinful soul than the word *confusion*. The famous seventh chapter of Romans can be summed up in that word. The victim is not one, but two persons, and these two are not equal; they are indeed at violent cross-purposes with each other. The will and the affections of this man who is two men are tangled up like live wires; and where they touch or cross, there are angry flashes and bursts of wasted energy.

Human society is simply confusion on a global scale; history is little more than a record of confusion, a chronicle of blunders and universal contradictions.

David did well to seek God's help in his troubles. When he faced confusion, he prayed, "Deliver me . . . and cause me to escape" (Psalm 71:2). God can deliver from confusion by establishing moral order within the life. When the eye becomes single, when the life becomes all one piece, inward antagonisms are abolished and internal harmony is restored.

It is not a wonder that there is so little of true joy among the sons of men. With the will at a perpetual stalemate, with the heart's purposes constantly at an irritating impasse, with the mind at wit's end and the whole life in a state of almost constant frustration, how can joy abide?

There is no way out of the woods except through full and quick surrender to the will of God. When such a surrender is made, God will soon bring order out of confusion. Peace is God's word, and it follows faith and obedience as the harvest follows the seed. But the whole will of God is necessary to peace; half measures will only increase the confusion.

25

The Opposing Spirits
of the Church and the World

THE WORLD and the true Church are by the nature of them irreconcilably opposed to each other. This opposition arises not from the things they do or do not do, but from two opposing spirits which dwell in them.

The world may differ from itself, may even quarrel with itself no end, but for all that it is of one piece still, moved by one spirit and indwelt by one soul. So the Church with its individual members is of one piece also, possessing the very nature of God and indwelt by the Holy Spirit

These two spirits are as far asunder as holiness and sin, and are forever in active opposition to each other; they can never be reconciled as long as each retains its essential nature. The once-born world can never forgive the twice-born Church her superior position. Always that which is born after the flesh will persecute that which is born of

49

the Spirit. The Spirit-born man can escape the world's hostility only by making compromises sufficiently vital to neutralize it. Unfortunately such also grieve and quench the Spirit within.

We escape the reproach of the cross (and thus the opposition of the world) by various diplomatic side-steppings which are labeled "wisdom" or "broad-mindedness" but which are in blunt actuality plain cowardice.

When a minor controversy arose among certain of the church bigwigs over the use in procession of Baring-Gould's hymn, "Onward, Christian Soldiers," the author ironically offered to change the line, "With the cross of Jesus going on before" to read, "With the cross of Jesus hid behind the door." We have become adept at concealing the cross and this while we honor it with our lips and preach it from our pulpits. And for this sin we pay a fearful price in weakness and sterility.

From being a radiant creature, "fair as the moon, clear as the sun, and terrible as an army with banners" (Song of Solomon 6:10), the Church has degenerated into a wizened crone, feared by none and actually pitied by the world that used to hate her. The world has in other days sought to use the Church where it could to further its political and economic ends, but so abject has her humiliation become that even the time-serving politicians no longer stoop to court her vote.

26

A Tribute to the Wife of Jesse

To the wife of Jesse the Bethlehemite, an obscure woman whose name we do not even know, the world owes a large debt of gratitude. She did us all a mighty favor, and then died, never dreaming that she had put an uncounted multitude of people under thanks to her forever.

When Samuel sought a king among the sons of Jesse, he rejected one after another of them till seven had passed by. Then he asked Jesse, "Are here all thy children?" Thanks to his wife, Jesse was able to answer, "There remaineth yet the youngest" (1 Samuel 16:11). Then little David stepped forward to become not only king, but the undisputed poet laureate of the kingdom of God.

We may thank God that Jesse's wife was not a modern woman with "advanced" ideas about the injustice of childbearing. What a sad loss it would have been to the world of believing men if she had balked at the hardships of a large family and had refused to bear that eighth boy!

It is evident from the record that David did not rate very high in the Jesse household. The birth of the seventh son was reason for congratulation, but David, who came along later, was unfortunately something of an anticlimax. The neighbors must have yawned and said, "Another one!" But it sometimes happens that way: nature experiments with the first seven and then comes forth with a David.

All Christendom has been enriched by the labors of Jesse's eighth son. The ancient goodwife, when she become the mother of David, became also the grandmother of the Twenty-third Psalm and of a host of other masterpieces of immortal hymnody. When the church sings, "The Lord's my Shepherd; I'll not want; He makes me down to lie," it is paying unwitting tribute to the wife of Jesse as well as offering worship to the Lord Jesus Christ.

When our summons comes and the creeping chill has numbed our lips so that we are able only to whisper, " . . . within Thy house forever," perhaps we can find a moment to remember gratefully a simple plain soul who once tried to do her duty by her generation. A little honest gratitude will be good for us, even in death.

27

God Suspends His
Judgment on Men

EVERY RANSOMED man owes his salvation to the
fact that during the days of his sinning God
kept the door of mercy open by refusing to accept
any of his evil acts as final.

The prodigal son is an illustration of this. The
enormity of the boy's sin was admitted by the father when he said plainly, "This my son was dead,
and is alive again" (Luke 15:24). The good man had
staggered under as cruel an attack upon paternal
love as has ever been recorded, but he never closed
his son's account. He never accepted his son's act as
conclusive, so he kept his heart and his door open.

The lone hope for a sinning man is that for a
while God will not accept his sinful conduct as de-
cisive. He will hold judgment in suspension, giving the sinner opportunity either to reverse
himself by repentance or to commit the final act
that will close the books against him forever.

God being who He is, the slightest act of wrongdoing must bring upon the sinner instant retribution were it not that, owing to the work of Christ in atonement, God is able justly to suspend justice. The cross does not destroy the deadly force of sins committed; unless they are removed by divine forgiveness they will return upon the perpetrator without mercy when the final act of evil springs the trap on him at last.

There comes a final act. This may not be the last act of the sinner's life, but rather the last one God will hold to be indecisive. It was so with King Saul: The Lord stopped all intercession for him, wrote him off as irreclaimable and closed the book. His doom was fixed the day God accepted his disobedience as the true index of his total character.

God gives us all the benefit of a long doubt; how long is His secret. It is a solemn thought that no one knows when he has crossed the line. On every city street and in quiet country lanes there are dead men walking whose fate has been settled long ago, but who, in their bold self-confidence, are callously unaware of it. The Judge has taken some last act of reckless sin as proof of what He may expect from them for the future. There remains for them only a certain fearful looking for judgment.

28

No One Is a Problem to God

Let no man imagine that he is a problem to God.

For him to do so is to assume that he is very much greater than he is in fact and to claim for himself powers which he does not in reality possess.

It is a none too subtle form of egotism to picture ourselves as great sinners, letting our imagination mount till we see ourselves strong and dangerous rebels, after the likeness of the Satan of Milton's *Paradise Lost,* actually threatening the security of the throne of God. We thus dramatize ourselves to hide our pitiful weakness.

That a man, by his sin, may ruin himself and greatly injure others is true. His sin, when seen in relation to himself and others, is great; but when set over against the boundless power and limitless resources of the Deity, it is as nothing at all.

Our theology is too much colored by our secret self-admiration. We picture God as draining the riches of heaven and consuming the last ounce of His strength to save us. This gives us a highly enjoyable feeling that we are capable of mighty world-shaking deeds so terrible that even God respects our power to do evil. The lurid overcoloring of pulpit rhetoric has worked to destroy the truth of God's sovereignty and to greatly overstate man's prowess as a sinning rebel.

A man may sin to the limit of his ability and still be no great problem to the Deity. "But where sin abounded, grace did much more abound" (Romans 5:20).

God is infinite and man is finite, which is to say that every man's sin, however terrific it may seem to him, must have a limit, while God's grace can have none. Always God must be out ahead, or He would not be God.

Let us put our pride under our feet and admit frankly that our sins are not big nor mighty nor noble. For my own part I will admit that my own sins have related me more nearly to the roach than to the rampant lion. There is nothing romantic about sin. It is a sordid and shameful thing practiced by moral cads so weak that they take advantage of God's kindness to defy Him and so cowardly that they run whining to Him for help when trouble comes.

29

Enemy #1: The Flesh

OF THE three enemies who compose that ancient trinity of evil—the world, the flesh and the devil—the toughest and most dangerous is the flesh.

The world and the devil are deadly foes, but for their power over us they depend altogether upon their ability to enlist the flesh against us. Through the door of the flesh only can they enter to do us harm.

What gives the flesh its terrific power is its dogged persistence, from childhood to old age; never for a second relaxing its vigilance, but worrying, strafing, sniping, mauling continually day after day, hour after hour to the end. It can change its form with every changing condition and fit its demands to every changing mood—sadness, gladness, remorse, fear, hope and even devotion. Each time we think it has been destroyed it comes up again under some new shape from some surprise direction.

With the flesh there is no such virtue as shame. Its impudence is incredible. It will not hesitate brazenly to follow its victim into the very sanctuary and to kneel along with him while he communes with his God. Let some prayer be answered, and the flesh will be there to suggest pride; let the answer be delayed, and it will suggest doubt. In the moment of utter self-abasement the flesh will cause the heart to feel a surge of carnal satisfaction with its own progress in holiness.

The flesh never dies while the victim lives. Cruel, determined, it stalks us to the end. Let a man hope that old age will destroy it, and he will be disappointed to find it there at the close of life polluting the last feeble stirrings of nature with its foul presence.

From the flesh there is no way of escape known to men under the sun. But still there is no reason for us Christians to despair. There is a way of release from its tyranny. It is by the cross of Jesus. The flesh dies before the terror of Calvary. God wills that we should be by faith completely identified with Christ in His act of dying. That ends the bondage of the flesh. The power to live free from it comes from the Holy Ghost. "For the law of the Spirit of life in Christ Jesus hath made me free from the law of sin and death" (Romans 8:2).

30

Dead Works and Vain Words

EVERY MAN should see to it that his words and deeds have the germ of life in them.

There are "dead works" and there are "vain words." Tragedy and loss attend them. Such words when spoken are lost; such works when done are wasted. Yet as strict an account must be made of them as if they had been living words and fertile deeds.

It is no intentional aspersion upon any church to say that much in religion is dead. The year-round activities of many churches are no more than a succession of dead works and vain words.

When I say that a church is dead, I do not mean only that its members are apathetic and slow to respond to the promptings of the Spirit. I mean something more terrible than that; I mean that its words and deeds have not the Spirit of life in them.

There are religious persons who have the name of Christ but whose spirit is the spirit of Adam.

They belong to the old order which perishes, not to the new order of life in Christ Jesus. The point is not that they are good or bad but that they are dead. Their direction is wrong; they are on their way to the grave, not on their way out of it.

It is not that I plant, but what I plant that matters. A man could plant glass beads for a lifetime and have nothing to show for his trouble; or he can, as did the famous "Johnny," plant apple seeds, and future generations will rise up to call him blessed.

Christ makes the difference between death and life, always and everywhere. He is the Prince of Life, and whatever He touches lives. The fabled Midas had a magic power which made everything he touched turn to gold. It is no fable, but wondrously true and real, that the power to give life belongs to Christ. Nothing He touches can ever die, and whatever is dead has only to be touched by Him and it lives again forever.

We who bear the name of Christ should give ourselves no rest till we are sure that we possess also the Spirit of Christ. "Now if any man have not the Spirit of Christ, he is none of his" (Romans 8:9). Without that Spirit no man can speak a living word or do an immortal deed.

31

Our Twisted World

I T IS a curiously twisted world where the matters of greatest import habitually receive the least attention, where care and pains are bestowed lavishly upon things that matter least, where pains and care diminish as the business in hand becomes increasingly more vital to the welfare of the individual who is engaged in it.

To thus characterize our human world is not exaggeration. Look at the record.

The most important thing in the world is our right relation to God, yet it is the business we attend to last. The most vital use we can make of our powers of speech is prayer, yet praying is the thing we do last and least. The book that could contribute most to our lasting welfare is the Bible, yet the average person never reads the Bible, and the relatively few who do read it read in the course of a year acres of newspaper to inches of Bible.

The knowledge of God is the most glorious

treasure anyone could possess, yet in most civilized countries there is but one institution engaged in promoting that knowledge, and even that institution is not working very hard at it.

Certainly religion is of greater importance than amusement, yet the average neighborhood movie theater is packed seven days a week, and the neighborhood church does well to get a fair crowd at its one or two weekly services.

We live in this world but a few years and in the next one forever, yet we think of this world almost all the time and of the next one scarcely once a year. The one experience we are sure we must face is death (and curiously enough, it is the only one we have a lifetime to prepare for), and yet it is the one experience we are least ready for when it comes.

Add to this the strange derangement that will lead men to slave through long weary years to win a posthumous fame which they, being dead, can never enjoy. Add to that the almost incredible fact that the whole instinct of the race is for life, and yet men constantly engage in wholesale killing to settle some question that might have been settled in twenty minutes in perfect amity if the ones involved had been morally sane.

It looks as if that cruel cynic, the devil, has done a pretty thorough job of wrecking the race.

32

Tender Christians

I THINK no good can come from trying to hide the fact that Christians are a temperamental lot, that religious people are often sensitive and high-strung to a degree not known to the sons and daughters of this world.

The explanation for this is easy. The people of the world are tougher minded and less painfully aware of the moral illogic within the Adamic social structure. Like unskilled musicians they do not know that their instrument is out of tune, and thus are cushioned against the moral shock of the discordant world about them. They have grown thick hides as a protection against each other, and they are not easily injured. They can engage in loud altercations, hurl coarse insults and feel none the worse for it.

Not so the Christian. He has learned the sweetness of his Lord's fellowship, and his heart has known the quiet ways of peace. The misunderstandings and abuses which he must sometimes endure pain him deeply. He cannot shake off the feeling that he is to be blamed for it, that he has failed his Savior somewhere and brought reproach upon the Cause. This makes for much suffering and sorrow of heart in the course of a lifetime.

We should not be too much troubled about this. The saints have suffered always, and much of their suffering is a compliment to their godliness. They have been out of joint with their times. They have insisted upon keeping their hearts alive and their consciences awake while others slept the sleep of moral insensibility. They have insisted upon being realists as well as idealists and have refused to have any truck with shadows. The world has made them pay well for their honesty.

Another thing that keeps many Christians on edge is the painful consciousness of their own imperfection. They feel within them an urge to be holy; they hear an insistent call that will not let them rest. Theirs is the pain of the process, theirs is the penalty of every spiritual aspiration.

Let us not waste pity on the saints for their sorrows; rather let us emulate them. They have chosen the better part. They could have sunk back, but they chose the nobler way.

33

The Mark of the Brother in Christ

IN THIS world of earthbound men there is still found, thank God, an election of grace. There are still a few who desire to follow the Lamb.

These favored ones may be by nature no better than the rest of mankind, but from somewhere there has come to them a weary dissatisfaction, a mighty discontent. Their hearts will not be satisfied with pottage; they cry for "the true bread from heaven" (John 6:32) whereof if a man eat he shall never hunger.

They are a varied lot, these elect souls, as different from each other as the flowers and the field are different, as the trees of the forest or the stars in the heaven above. Yet they are alike in one thing; one mark they bear which makes them kin wherever they are found: It is their dissatisfaction with this world and their huge desire after God and the world to come.

There is a glorious catholicity of the saints, a mystic brotherhood of the farsighted who have long been straining their eyes to catch a glimpse of the King in His beauty in the land that is very far off. With great joy and deep humility I claim membership in that brotherhood. This is the oldest and largest church in the world; it is the church of the cross-smitten, of the God-enamored.

As the years go on, I am coming to care less and less about any man's denominational ties. Let a man have a faraway look in his eyes, let him bow his head and whisper the ever-blessed name of Jesus, and he is my brother whatever his name may be. And he is my brother whether he will admit it or not. If by some bit of unfortunate education he may believe his church to be the only one and consign me to perdition because I am not in it, I will still own him a member of the family of God if I find in his life the marks of the cross and in his eyes the long look that reveals the man of faith.

If we could only rise above our prejudices, we should see that all God's children bear a family resemblance to each other. And we should see also that no matter how loudly a man may protest his faith in Christ, no matter how often he may be found before the altar, if he have not the sign of the cross in his heart, he is for all his religion a man most miserable, a soul lost in the night.

34

The Unity of the God-Smitten

THERE IS a fellowship within a fellowship—a sort of wheel in the middle of a wheel—which gathers to itself all who are of its spirit in every church in every land and every age. Its members are the God-smitten, those who have heard the Voice speaking within them and have caught a glimpse, however fleeting, of the glory of God.

These have a remarkable likeness to each other wherever they are found. Discounting their imperfections, admitting their mistakes and weaknesses, they are yet found to be a people apart, separated from the rest of mankind not by legal prohibitions but by a spirit which dwells within them.

They who compose this fellowship have never been herded into any one organization; they have no earthly head, pay no dues, hold no conventions and keep no minutes, yet they recognize each other instantly when they meet by a kind of secret sign which the Spirit has placed within their hearts.

These have been in the Presence and will never be the same again. They know a holy reverence, a wondrous sense of sacredness that rises at times to transports of delight. Their garments smell of myrrh and aloes and cassia, a gift from their Bridegroom and King who came walking out of the Ivory Palaces, trailing clouds of glory, to win them for Himself.

These hail each other across the oceans and down the years. Over the barriers set up in ignorance by stubborn men to separate the children of God, they leap to clasp each others' hands and share together the feast of holy bread and wine.

Often their narrow theologies divide them from each other; but when they pray and sing, their essential unity is revealed. The Protestant will sing with joyous tears the songs of Faber and Newman who were Catholics. The Armenian will worship God with the hymns of Newton and Toplady who were Calvinists, and no one feels any inconsistency or embarrassment, for it is the heart that sings, and it is the heart that recognizes the marks of the cross that make of many one.

Could it be that it is here, rather than in some external unity, that the prayer of Jesus finds its fulfillment: "That they all may be one" (John 17:21)?

35

Measuring Spirituality by Public Prayers

T HE DEPTHS of a man's spirituality may be known quite accurately by the quality of his public prayers.

Bible prayers remain the most perfect examples of what prayer should be to please most our heavenly Father. How bold they are, yet how respectful; how intimate, yet how deeply reverent.

Those who heard Luther's prayers have told us of the tremendous effect they often had upon the listeners. He would begin in moving humility, his spirit facedown in utter self-abnegation, and sometimes rise to a boldness of petition that would startle the hearers.

There is among us today a pseudo-mysticism which affects a tender intimacy with God but lacks that breathless awe which the true worshiper must always feel in the presence of the Holy God. This simpering spirit sometimes expresses itself in religious baby talk wholly unworthy of those who are addressing the Most High.

To hear a so-called Christian cooing in a voice indelicately familiar, addressing words of saccharine sweetness to one whom he or she calls "Jesus dear," is a shocking experience for anyone who has once seen heaven opened and stood speechless before the Holy Presence. No one who has ever bowed before the Burning Bush can thereafter speak lightly of God, much less be guilty of levity in addressing Him.

When Horace Bushnell prayed in the field under the night sky, his friend who knelt by his side drew in his arms close to his body. "I was afraid to stretch out my hands," he said, "lest I touch God."

While prayers are not addressed to the listeners, they are, nevertheless, meant to be heard by them and should be made with that knowledge frankly in mind. Paul makes this perfectly clear in his first Corinthian epistle. Finney had much to say about this also, as did certain others of the religious great.

We would do well in these days of superficialities in religion to rethink the whole matter of public prayer. It will lose nothing of spiritual content from being subjected to prayerful thought and reverent criticism.

36

Reflections on the Grace of God

INCREASING KNOWLEDGE of God's ways and works, especially His wise and tender treatment of His redeemed children, fills me with ever mounting degrees of admiration and praise. It is becoming every day easier to understand experientially the hosannas and hallelujahs which make up such a large portion of the sacred Scriptures. They are the normal response of the heart to the manifold goodness of God, and it would, in fact, be hard to understand their omission if they were not found there.

While I have no doubt that the grace which has followed me since my boyhood will continue with me while I live on earth and for an eternity after, I have enjoyed already enough of God's benefits to supply me with matter for constant praise for at least a thousand years to come. If God were to close my account tomorrow and refuse any longer to honor me with His favors, the circumstances of His grace to me so far would require that I should still thank Him unceasingly with tears of honest gratitude.

I am sincerely grateful that He has allowed me to look upon the pages of His holy Word and thus enabled me to think His thoughts after Him. I am thankful that He allowed me to walk where He walked, if only for a brief time. I am glad, glad that He has let me hear His voice, even if the sound was but faint and indistinct; that He has allowed me to behold His glory, though the vision was but fleeting and dim. He has let me see, if only at a distance, a splendor, a light that never was on land or sea. He has let me call Him Father and has not drawn back in dismay at the imperfections He found and still finds in me.

All this He has done for me and more, for He has allowed me to speak His words to a few, to hold the torch of truth to the feet of at least a small number who were stumbling in the night. And if any word or work of mine has helped to save some child of God from sorrow or despair, then that too is all of unmixed grace and further cause of continual praise.

His salvation is as eternal as His own person. As long as God remains who and what He is, I shall remain an object of His love in Christ Jesus.

37

Christ Saves the Whole Person

THAT REFERENCE in Hebrews to the Word of
God being able to pierce even to "the divid-
ing asunder of soul and spirit" (Hebrews 4:12) has
led to some fantastic speculations about the state
of the believer in the day of Christ. Some have
held that our spirit may be saved and our souls
lost depending upon how severely we discipline
ourselves while under probation here on earth.

The notion that my spirit may be saved and my
soul lost presents to my prosaic mind a picture
which I find too grotesque for credence. Imagine
half a man floating around among the ransomed,
trying with only half his faculties to celebrate the
honors of the Creator. There's something wrong
there, and I suspect it is with the luxuriant imagination of some of our experts on obscure texts.

However easily we may think ourselves into
sections, we can never actually separate ourselves
into our component parts. Each of us is a unit, and
it was for us as such that God provided redemp-

tion. Christ died not for one part or another of the sinner, but for the whole man. Paul said the Son of God "loved me, and gave himself for me" (Galatians 2:20). That little word "me" embraced the whole magnificent personality of the apostle, everything he was or is or can be. The total of a redeemed being is in that one small word. Doctrinal soundness would seem to require that we think of people as whole persons as men and women, not as souls and spirits in danger of coming apart.

Faith in Christ is an all-inclusive act of the believer's being. It must include the soul, the spirit, the mind, the will and the affections. Anything less is a trick faith and not Bible faith at all.

Faith is the total response of the whole being to the Person of Christ. It is the flowering of the entire personality, the going out of the complete life Godward. The whole man believes or the whole man doubts; the whole man is lost or the whole man is saved.

This view (unless I am mistaken) represents the historic doctrinal position of evangelical Christianity. It seems to accord with common sense and square with the Bible itself. And it saves a lot of unprofitable figuring.

38

Believing Requires Obedience

I<small>T IS</small> easy to be orthodox in matters that are remote from us, that have no immediate bearing upon our lives. It is quite another thing to be orthodox in matters which intimately concern us, which "come home to our business and our bosoms."

A man may, for instance, believe the Mosaic account of creation, the stories of the flood and of Joshua's commanding the sun to stand still and experience no difficulty whatever. For, after all, he is neither better nor worse for believing those things. They make no moral demands upon him. He can believe them implicitly without altering his life.

He may go on to accept the whole record of the life and work of Christ as given in the New Testament. He may receive without question every doctrine taught by his church and yet be exactly the same man as he was before, the only slight difference being a small increase in the amount of his mental furniture.

Receiving the truth is not enough. The man who would know the power of the Christian faith must submit and obey. When our faith becomes obedient, the mighty energies of grace begin to operate.

We are always in danger of allowing teaching to substitute for living. Indoctrination is not regeneration and should never be mistaken for it. Thousands are turned out of confirmation classes each year who have never known the transforming power of the gospel. These go out to be lifelong anomalies, orthodox in creed, but untouched pagans in fact. They have absorbed the notion that to receive the creed concerning Christ is identical with receiving Christ. This is a costly and tragic error.

There is one sure way to escape the delusions of religion: Receive Christ as Lord of our lives and begin to obey Him in everything. Submit to the truth and let it search us. Submit and obey are hard and exacting words but necessary if we would be true Christians.

But actually there is nothing frightening about the demands of Christ. "For my yoke is easy, and my burden is light" (Matthew 11:30), He said to His disciples, and a great multitude could rise up today and say, "We have found it so."

39

No Grounds for Pride

THERE ARE few things which excite among mankind such humorous pity as the sight of a vain little man puffing himself up to try to hide his essential smallness.

A group of literary men were once reverently examining a watch which had belonged to the great Milton when the poet Wordsworth who sat among them solemnly took his own watch from his pocket and without a word passed it around the circle! Deeply as we may love the sweet poet of nature, he suffers in our eyes for that display of weakness.

It is when we enter the sanctuary of God, however, that pride takes on its ugliest and most offensive character. The angels veil their faces in His presence, but it is not uncommon to find two men of God quarreling over who gets the credit for some work performed ostensibly for the glory of God alone.

Three considerations should destroy pride forever within our breasts: the majesty of God, the enormity of our sins and the wonder of Christ's redeeming death. But so tenacious is the root of Adam that we are often proud even of our want of pride. It is not uncommon to see holy men defending their holiness with positive violence and resenting any doubt cast upon their perfections.

For a Christian to claim credit for any good work is a violation of the most elementary teachings of the New Testament. Two things are taught clearly there: that I can of myself do no good thing; and if any good deed is done, it is the Lord Himself who has done it. That should settle our pride of service for good, but in fact it is not so. We still love to bask in the praise that our Christian efforts bring us.

For a Christian to revel in the praise he is accorded for some good work is as logically askew as for a singer to rush out and take a bow for another singer's solo. It is a cheap form of robbery and must be exceedingly hateful to God.

The facts seem to dictate this position: If I did it, it is not good, however good it may seem to be; and its seeming to be good is all a snare and a delusion. If God did it, why should I boast of the accomplishment of another?

40

The Church's Most Harmful Sins

ALL SINS are hateful to God, but not all sins are equally injurious to the community of Christians we call the Church.

I hesitate to name the sins I have found most harmful to the life of the Church, for I do not find among them any of the old standbys which have served as whipping-boys for most of the evangelists since the days of Sam Jones.

The first one I would name is a bad disposition. By this I mean ill nature, churlishness, grouchiness in general. It is my opinion that this sin has caused more human anguish than any other on the blotter. Without it there would be never a quarrel, never a divorce, never a church split. To be forced to live in close association with an irascible grouch is hell enough for any man for one lifetime.

Next I would mention a complaining spirit. This has the same effect in a church as a set of spoiled, fretful quadruplets would have in a home; it makes things all but unbearable. Little wonder that the Lord destroyed the murmurers from among the Israelites.

Then comes selfishness. This manifests itself in a callous disregard for the rights of others. It is the exact opposite of that love which "seeketh not her own."

Next, stubbornness. This leads its possessor to stick to a point in blind unreason even if it ties up the work of God, divides brethren and ruins a church.

Self-importance is another of the enemies of the Church of Christ. It would be amusing to see little men strut about in the holy place were it not that we are witnessing a particularly offensive demonstration of the sin that caused the fall of Lucifer and has brought about the disintegration of many a fine church.

Harshness is next. Many a new convert has quit and gone back to Egypt after being wounded by some harsh-spirited Christian.

Lastly, a gossiping tongue. This is probably the deadliest of them all. It spreads the infection through the body and, as far as possible, poisons every member.

It would be interesting to know whether or not this list agrees with yours.

41

The Reality of Persecution

THE WARFARE of the Christian is like foreign missions, romantic to talk about but drably realistic to live through.

Foxe's Book of Martyrs provides a delightful thrill in the reading, but I doubt that any of the martyrs themselves enjoyed their dyings as much as we enjoy reading about them.

The habit of speaking always in highly colored figures when describing the Christian life has created an idealistic picture altogether unlike the life itself. Just as a battle as conceived by the civilian who reads about it differs from the mud and blood and dirt and unspeakable weariness of the real thing, so the Christian life as we all must live it is quite another thing from the joyous adventure of the "blood-washed pilgrim in shining garments clad" of whom we have heard in the familiar song.

There is need for greater realism in our Christian testimony. Those who follow the Lamb must face the hostility of the world, and we may be sure there will be nothing enjoyable in the world's displeasure.

The Word of God itself does not hedge the facts. "All that will live godly in Christ Jesus shall suffer persecution" (2 Timothy 3:12). So states the apostle frankly. But here again we have refused to allow the ugly word persecution to mean what it means. We have poetized it and covered it with a shimmering garment of soft sentiment. Consequently when a new convert first runs into the cold, harsh suffering he must endure for Christ's sake, he is not prepared to face it.

It is right here that many go back. They are neatly handled by those who have brought them to that pass. It is all simple. They are simply classified as backsliders. I wonder if they are so in fact. Are they not rather persons who have been persuaded to become Christians by false representation, and who, when they later see the whole picture, do not care for what they see?

In our eagerness to make converts we are under constant temptation to hide from our hearers the fact that the Christian life is not a pleasurable religious game, but a life of repentance, self-crucifixion, humiliation and rejection.

42

Coddled or Crucified?

T HE SPIRITUAL giants of old would not take their religion the easy way nor offer unto God that which cost them nothing. They sought not comfort but holiness, and the pages of history are still wet with their blood and their tears.

We now live in softer times. Woe unto us, for we have become adept in the art of comforting ourselves without power.

Almost every radical effort of the Holy Ghost to lead us forth to heroic self-crucifixion is now partied with a fine sophistry drawn from—of all sources—the Word of God itself. I hear it often these days. The trick is to say, half comically, amused at our own former ignorance, "Once I was distressed over my lack of power, my spiritual sterility, as I then thought; but one day the Lord said to me, 'My child, etc., etc.' " Then follows a quotation direct from the mouth of the Lord condoning our weakness and self-coddling. Thus the very authority of divine inspiration is given to what is obviously but the defensive reasoning of our own hearts.

Those who will justify themselves in that kind of dodging are not likely to be much affected by anything I can say or write. No one is so dead as the man who has turned the very thunders of judgment into a lullaby to soothe him into sound sleep and has made the sacred Scriptures themselves a hiding place from reality.

But to those who will hear I would say with all the urgency at my command: Though the cross of Christ has been beautified by the poet and the artist, the avid seeker after God is likely to find it the same savage implement of destruction it was in the days of old. The way of the cross is still the pain-wracked path to spiritual power and fruitfulness.

So do not seek to hide from it. Do not accept an easy way. Do not allow yourself to be patted to sleep in a comfortable church, void of power and barren of fruit. Do not paint the cross nor deck it with flowers. Take it for what it is, as it is, and you will find it the rugged way to death and life. Let it slay you utterly. Seek God. Seek to be holy and fear none of those things which thou shalt suffer.

43

The Harm of Religious Chatter

M OST CHRISTIANS, I find, help each other very little in ordinary conversation, and often do each other much harm. There are few who can talk for any length of time without descending to speech that is not only unprofitable but positively harmful.

For myself, I get little help from the fellowship of Christians, and I am sure that up to this time they have received very little help from mine.

This is a flaw in our lives which should be dealt with seriously. It often happens that all the good effect of a service will be destroyed by light and unworthy conversation after the meeting. This is a sad fault, for the ministry of any church should be no more than a public expression of the pure spirituality which is the regular day by day life of such as are a part of it.

The minister himself should simply carry into the pulpit on Sunday the same spirit which has characterized him all week long. He should not need to adopt another voice nor speak in a different tone. The subject matter would necessarily differ from that of his ordinary conversation, but the mood and attitude expressed in his sermons should be identical with his daily living.

Harmful or vain speech blocks revival and grieves the Spirit more than we are likely to realize. It destroys the accumulative effect of spiritual impressions and makes it necessary each Sunday to recapture the devotional mood which has been lost during the week. Thus we are compelled constantly to do over again the work of last week and to retake ground lost by unprofitable conversation.

It is not desirable that we form the habit of constant religious chatter when we meet with our friends. There is no surer proof of our basic levity of character than the careless way religion is often discussed among us. I do not here plead for more religious talk. Religious shoptalk can be as dull and boring as any other shoptalk; and what is worse, it may become insincere and meaningless.

The ideal to aim at is a chaste, natural and love-washed conversation at all times whether we are discussing things on earth or things in heaven.

44

Deciding to Exercise Faith

To the seeker after God faith is so vitally important that its value can hardly be exaggerated.

"Without faith it is impossible to please him" (Hebrews 11:6). Until faith is present, God sternly refuses to deal with even the most earnest soul. Unbelief seals off the seeker and effectively blocks his access to God. With the unbelieving man God will simply have nothing to do.

Apart from prayer there is probably no Bible doctrine which receives so much attention as does faith, yet there are few things about which we know less.

We must not, however, be troubled because we are not able to define it. Scarcely one of the great realities by which we live can be defined. Love, light, life—who can even remotely approach to a definition of these? Yet they are more vital to our existence than any of the material things which can be subjected to close definition. Such as these must be experienced to be understood, and at best only the heart understands. The intellect is too clumsy to lay hold of their secret.

The common effort to induce faith by artificial stimulation is an evil and should be abandoned. The pitiful struggling with a text in an effort to prove to a seeker that he has faith reveals a complete misunderstanding of the whole matter. It is the work of the teacher to present the truth to the mind of the hearer; it is the work of the Spirit to create faith. When a man has faith he knows it. He needs no eager logic jockey to manipulate him into a pleasant mood.

The cause of unbelief in the heart is always sin in the life. Let the seeker deal with his sin radically, and he is not likely thereafter to experience much difficulty in believing. For believing is not an act of the intellect. It is an act of the will. It is a moral thing, not a mental one.

Yet it is comforting to know that God, if He is to help us at all, must respond to a very imperfect faith, for it is such a faith that we all bring Him when first we begin the life of trust. The first simple faith that lays hold of Christ for eternal life is not of the same quality and strength as that which develops later by long exercise and earnest prayer.

45

How Does the Christian Measure Importance?

THOUGHTS ON Peter and the lame man at the Gate Beautiful:

The healing of the lame man brought a great crowd together. Peter took advantage of the opportunity to preach Christ to those who were thus assembled.

Here we learn the Lord's own advertising secret: It is to excite interest and focus attention by the sheer wonder of His mighty acts of deliverance. A healed lame man is the best copy any advertiser could wish. Peter's crowd did not cost him one dime in hard cash.

Peter's pecuniary status was exactly zero-minus. He operated pretty literally on a shoestring. If he were living today, he would be scorned by our current religious promoters and ignored by the leaders as small-time and visionless.

Two other counts against the apostle as judged

by modern standards are these: He had never been anywhere, and he did not know anyone. His only contact with the bigwigs of his day was in the police court where he went by their summons to answer to the charge of preaching the resurrection.

Peter had never been anywhere and did not know anyone! Wait—he had been in the Upper Room, and he knew Jesus. Would that qualify him? As far as I am concerned it would. It would be a wonderful thing if all our evangelists had the same qualifications. It would fit more nearly the New Testament pattern.

No matter how loudly we protest our faith, we are not apostolic as long as we continue to see things backward from the way the apostles saw them. As long as our test of importance is the same as the world's, our spirit is certainly the spirit of the world.

Peter said, "Look on us. . . . Why look ye . . . on us?" (Acts 3:4, 12). He made their looking on him to be a brief prelude to their eternal looking on Jesus. The art of being somebody in order to be nobody that Christ may be everything is all but lost to us today. Now we see either a morbid humility which dare not say, "Look on us" or a brazen egotism which will not say, "Why look ye on us?" A saint courageous enough to command attention and humble enough to redirect it to Christ is a rarity.

46

The Public Reading of Scripture

W HEN PAUL exhorted Timothy to "give atten-
dance to reading" (1 Timothy 4:13), the
context shows that he had in mind the public
reading of the Scriptures.

The Old Testament also gives us numerous examples of the public reading of the Word of God.
It appears to have constituted an important part of
the worship of the Jews at various periods.

However other things in our churches may differ, there is one matter upon which there should
be full agreement and uniformity of practice: the
reading aloud of the very words of the Lord in our
Sunday services.

The minister in charge of the weekly meetings
should take pains to see that the Word is read
before the congregation in a voice clear enough
to be understood and loud enough to be heard
by all. To take great care for the sermon, and
then for public reading grab the Bible and hast-
ily turn to the first passage that looks inviting is

to place the sermon above the Word of God itself.

One method of reading which is of great value is the responsive reading of the Psalms from the Bible itself. This encourages the people to bring their Bibles and also allows them to participate in the reading, both of which habits are splendid for spiritual development.

So far as my experience has gone I would conclude that few people know how to read the Scriptures with any degree of proficiency. Too often there is a tendency to swallow our tones, to misplace emphasis, to fall into a sing-song voice or to stumble over the proper names. This should be corrected early in our Christian lives, and the art of clear, skillful reading should be perfected. It will yield wonderful returns.

To hear William Jennings Bryan read a favorite passage from the Scriptures was an event in the life of anyone fortunate enough to have had that privilege. He labored to read God's Word in a manner worthy of its Author. Though we cannot hope to read with the organ-tone beauty of the great Commoner, we can improve our reading ability several hundred percent if we but determine to do so. And the Church of God will profit from our toil.

47

We Dare Not Preach a
Superficial Gospel

W<small>E ARE</small> too superficial these days in our dealings with religious inquirers.

Altar services are often rushed through in noisy
haste, with a little sniffle on the part of the seeker
being accepted as proof that a work of God has
been done. We are so pitifully eager to get people
"through" that we encourage them to "believe"
and "praise" when as yet they are still in darkness.

I believe we owe it to the souls of men to check
on our work sometimes to see whether or not our
labors have been in vain. Some would shrink from
this as being irreverent and unbelieving. Is, then,
the work of God in salvation such a fragile thing
that it withers before the glance of a clear eye? I
think not. When Christ raised Lazarus the man
himself was there as a visible proof of the miracle.

We dare not be satisfied with any evangelism,
however well organized and widely publicized, till

it begins to produce results we can "handle" a week or a year later.

Lives permanently transformed—these are the final proofs of a work, whether it be of God or not. Whatever will not meet this acid test of permanence is a delusion, nothing less.

The same tragic shallowness is found in a certain type of personal evangelism where the stress is laid upon the mere act of "accepting" Christ as the only requirement for salvation. No mention is made of the rights which the Lord claims in the life of the individual following his supposed act of faith, as repentance, obedience, separation, cross-bearing.

This quasi-Christianity was preached to millions of our servicemen during the late war, with what sad effects only God can know. Thousands of frightened and heartsick boys were fed this emasculated gospel; and because they gave verbal assent to it they were assured that everything was well with their souls, even though they were in reality totally blind to the whole will of God and to all the claims of Christ.

Some of us are going to answer for these betrayed souls in that day when the Lord comes to judge the secrets of all men's hearts.

48

The Holy Spirit Is Christ Among Us

PENTECOST DID not come and go; Pentecost came and stayed. Chronologically the day may be found on the historic calendar; dynamically it remains with us still in all its fullness of power.

Today is the day of Pentecost. With the blessed Holy Spirit there is no yesterday nor tomorrow; there is only an everlasting now. And since He is altogether God, enjoying all the attributes of the Godhead, there is with Him no elsewhere; He inhabits an eternal here. He is that whose center is everywhere, whose bound is nowhere. It is impossible to leave His presence (though it is possible to have Him withdraw the manifestation of that presence).

Our insensibility to the presence of the Spirit is one of the greatest losses our unbelief and preoccupation have cost us. We have made Him a tenet in our creed, we have enclosed Him in a religious word, but we have known Him very little in personal experience. Satan has hindered us all he could by raising conflicting opinions about the Spirit, by making Him a topic for hot and uncharitable debate between Christians. In the meanwhile our hearts crave Him, and we hardly know what the craving means.

It would help us if we could remember that the Spirit is Himself God, the very true Nature of the Godhead subsisting in a form that can impart Himself to our consciousness. We know only as much of the other Persons of the Trinity as He reveals to us. It is His light upon the face of Christ which enables us to know Him. It is His light within us which enables us to understand the Scriptures. Without Him the Word of truth is only darkness.

The Spirit is sent to be our Friend, to guide us over the long way home. He is Christ's own Self come to live with us, allowing Him to fulfill His word, "Lo, I am with you alway" (Matthew 28:20) even while He sits at the right hand of the Majesty in the heavens.

It will be a new day for us when we put away false notions and foolish fears and allow the Holy Spirit to fellowship with us as intimately as He wants to do, to talk to us as Christ talked to His disciples by the Sea of Galilee. After that there can be no more loneliness, only the glory of the never-failing Presence.

49

Keep the Donkeys Out!

IN JUSTICE to the hero of this story it should be told, though we are a bit late in the telling of it. A certain Chicago church, known to run to the sensational, put on during the holidays an elaborate religious play. One scene called for the entrance onto the improvised stage of a little donkey. When it came the donkey's cue, to the embarrassment of the director and the huge delight of the audience, the noble little fellow stubbornly refused to mount the rostrum. Neither coaxing nor persuasion could move him, and the perspiring director had finally to give it up as a bad job. Whether the donkey objected to having them make a bigger donkey out of him than he had been before, or whether he felt a reverent sense of his unfittedness for the pulpit is not known.

Not all details of the story have been supplied me, and I am unable to say how the show got on without the donkey, though I assume that some other member of the cast substituted for him and probably acted his part quite as naturally as he himself could have done. But I am for the donkey. He should be pensioned for life and should go down in history along with the famous beast of Balaam's day as having more piety than the publicity-hunting prophets of his time.

Religious shows leave a bad flavor. When they enter the holy place, they come perilously near to offering strange fire to the Lord. At their worst they are sacrilege; always they are unnecessary; and at their best they are a poor substitute for prayer and the Holy Ghost. Church plays are invariably cheap and amateurish, and in addition to grieving the Holy Ghost, those who attend them are cheated by getting wretchedly poor entertainment for their money.

On the pulpit of a famous mission appears the text: "Sirs, we would see Jesus," a gentle reminder to the speaker to keep to his subject, Christ and Him crucified. When the pulpit is used for any other purpose than to set forth the Word of God, the glory has departed. Let us keep the Bible in the pulpit, and as far as possible keep the donkeys out!

50

The Humble Simplicity
of the God-Conscious

CHRISTIANITY AT its best is sweetly uncon-scious of itself. It serves God in frank sim-plicity and lives from within with never a doubt of its full right to exist. It does not mince nor apologize. It accepts itself with uncritical inno-cence and gazes out on life with the sincerity of a child.

There is today a branch of self-conscious Chris-tianity which claims to be the true faith of the New Testament, but unfortunately there is about it very little of the childlike. Those who have ab-sorbed its spirit are neither completely happy nor are they wholly free. Their testimony is defiant and their total character defensive.

Some time ago I attended a meeting where the tone was one of cocky contempt for modernism. The leader chose songs about the blood of Christ as a protest against those who did not believe in it.

This was not an inference made by me but was several times mentioned by the leader. As much as I owe to the blood of Christ, I yet could not join in the singing.

The victims of this school of self-conscious orthodoxy can never say in glad surprise, "My Lord and my God!" They must always say, "In spite of what some people think, I will be true to the old Book—'My Lord and my God!' "

That kind of religious exercise is not the spontaneous expression of what Carlyle called "transcendent wonder" in the presence of the wonderful One. It is rather a dig at the enemy whose feared and hated image is always visible out of the corner of the worshiper's eye.

The man who has once met God face to face is not likely to be skittish about what others think of him. He is more likely to be so acutely God-conscious that he merely smiles absentmindedly at their criticisms.

An overbearing, bullying testimony is never a proof of real faith. Rather is it an evidence of deep uncertainty and lack of a satisfying spiritual experience. The man whose faith is on the defensive must be always explaining to the opposer or else brazenly defying him. The man of true faith does neither. He simply lives his life in God, and that life is its own justification.

51

A Potpourri of Tozer

Editor's Note

Occasionally, Tozer's early columns in The Alliance Weekly *consisted of separate paragraphs on various topics rather than a complete essay. The best of these "mini-sermons" are reprinted here for your edification. Some of them have also appeared in* In Pursuit of God, *a biography of Tozer.*

PERPETUAL DISCIPLES are a reproach to any teacher. We should teach men and women how to walk alone, looking only to God for support. The quicker they can get along without us, the better we have done our job as teachers. The temptation to make ourselves indispensable is very strong, but we must learn to enjoy the pain of seeing our disciples catch up with us or even pass us on the way.

S OME PEOPLE spend all their time on a kind of doctrinal trapeze and never come down long enough to learn how to walk with God. Out our way they swing by their toes on the flying bar of divine sovereignty, turn a double somersault, catch hold of the eternal decrees and come up bowing on the mystery of predestination. It may be good exercise (though I suspect a little strenuous for the average heart), but I have not noticed that it makes them any holier or more Christlike. The wise words of Thomas à Kempis should not be forgotten: "It is better to *feel* compunction than to know the definition thereof."

I LIKE A pipe organ in a church, especially where the preacher is a modernist. I enjoy counting the pipes and trying to guess which palm the console is hidden behind while the preacher distills his learned doubts over the congregation.

D R. GRIFFITH THOMAS' famous dictum, "First be spiritual, then be natural," should be written on every pulpit where the man of God cannot help seeing it while he speaks. Artificiality is a common ministerial fault and one that goes far to undo the very work the minister is trying to accomplish. It is hard to preserve a proper spirit of worship while listening to the man addicted to saying "yea-a-a" when he means "yes" and "na-a-a-y" when he means "no," or stopping frequently to reassure his hearers with a tender "beloved," or shouting, red faced and hard-voiced, that their sins are breaking his heart.

MANY PREACHERS have occasion to be thankful for the Revised Version margin. It is verily a present help in time of trouble. But I am always suspicious of any sermon that has to use crutches. If there is not plain Scripture enough to support the idea, better throw it out; it probably is not so anyway.

WE DO not hear so much about religious debates these days. They seem to be on the wane, and the sooner they cease altogether, the better it will be for everybody. I am opposed to religious debates on half-a-hundred counts, the chief objection being that they fail to convince anybody. Each one comes to the meeting bringing his prejudices along with him and proceeds to vote exactly as he had intended to vote before he had heard the evening's arguments. We are called to preach the Bible, not to prove it. The Holy Ghost is all the proof we need.

IF ONE-TENTH of one percent of the prayers made in any American city on any Sabbath day were answered, the world would see its greatest revival come with the speed of light. We seem to have gotten used to prayers that produce nothing. God still hears prayer and all the promises are still good, yet we go on at a pretty dying rate. Can someone tell us the answer?

I N A cemetery at Oberlin, Ohio, there stands a simple stone marking the grave of the great evangelist Charles G. Finney. His name, the dates of his birth and death and a verse of Scripture are engraved on the stone. There is nothing more. This prince with God needs no imposing granite to tell his praises to the passing years. His fame is secure in the unforgetting hearts of ten thousand American Christians. But in the light of what he was and of what our country has become, there is a tender yearning in the verse engraved there which every true Christian and patriot will deeply feel: "The Lord be with us as He was with our fathers. May He not leave us nor forsake us."

A PREACHER NOT long ago announced that he would have for his subject the next Sunday evening, "Don't Tear Your Shirt." He took for his text these words, "Rend your hearts and not your garments," and preached on repentance. It is that kind of thing that makes atheists. To approach a solemn subject in such a flippant manner is inexcusable. It is time the Christian public goes on a gracious and dignified strike against such comic-strip parody of gospel preaching. A listener said of

Moody, "He was the most deadly in earnest man I ever heard." He adorned the message he preached.

N OT LONG ago I heard a sweet-faced, pure young girl get up in meeting and testify that God had saved her from the very depths and dregs of iniquity, or words to that effect. Her whole voice and bearing bore evidence to her sheltered life, and her testimony, for that reason, had no meaning for anyone with an eye to facts. She was not consciously lying, and her motive was no doubt good, but she was trying to glorify God by giving someone's else testimony. No good claiming to be a Magdalene unless you have been one; no good claiming deliverance from seven devils when you have had only one. Do not overdo your devils. The grace of God will not suffer from your telling the exact truth.

H AVE YOU ever noticed how the space devoted to church advertising in the newspapers shrinks after Easter? The devil must enjoy a diabolical chuckle when he sees how some churches run to seasons in religion. In deference to tradition I am willing to concede that there is some value in the observation of Lent, but I have never gone in for it much myself. Of course, it is a convenience to be able to compress a whole year's service to the Lord into six weeks. But then again it must be a bothersome thing to have to hunt around for a calendar when you want to pray to find out whether prayer is in season. And imagine getting hold of an old calendar by mistake and praying sometime when it did not count!

I USED TO be afraid of learned unbelievers. Their smiling superiority led me to believe that they knew a great deal more than they do, and their summary dismissal of religion made me uneasy. What if, after all, they knew too much to accept Christianity, and I accepted it only because I was ignorant?

That question troubled me once, but it troubles me no more. A closer acquaintance with the opinions and arguments of these men proves to me that they are unbelievers out of prejudice, not as a result of any great knowledge they possess. It is in fact amazing how little some of them really know.

I am fully convinced that no man on earth knows or can know enough to seriously threaten the foundations of our faith. The most that honest scholarship can ever do is to strip away some of the moss that clings to the strong pillars upon which the Church of God rests.

D OWN BY the Chicago city dump a few families manage to exist, sharing their poor hovels with the rats and subsisting mainly on what they can salvage from the refuse thrown away by the city's millions.

A zealous young Christian worker heard about these people and determined to take the gospel to them. He collected from the dump large pieces of sheet metal and other material and built a crude church. He opened a Sunday school and established preaching services. That was some time ago, and God has since crowned his efforts with success. Today that church, probably the strangest institution in the world, operates on a weekly schedule, ministering the Word of Life to human beings who would be considered outcasts even in the slums.

Not many would care to go there, but it is certain that the Lord of glory has attended every service since the work began. He will have jewels even from the dumps. "Though ye have lien among the pots, yet shall ye be as the wings of a dove covered with silver, and her feathers with yellow gold" (Psalm 68:13).

THE GREATEST danger we face from this machine age is that we will become engrossed with mechanical gadgets and forget we have hearts. Man cannot live by bread alone nor by machinery alone. The heart must be nurtured. For this reason the prophet and the poet are more important to a nation than the engineer or the inventor. Longfellow and Whittier have meant more to us than Edison or Ford. Burns' songs have meant more to Scotland than Watts' steam engine.

SOMEONE HAS advanced the idea that if we would have a revival, we should begin to sing; that revivals always come on the wings of song. It is true that revivals and song always go together, but the song is the effect of the revival, never the cause of it. Men are not revived because they sing; they sing because they are revived. It is coldness of heart that has caused us to lose the joy and zest from our singing. The revived heart will soon burst into song.

SAMUEL BOGGS, late head of the Gideons, was a great lay preacher. He used to preach a thought-provoking sermon called "Unknown Disciples." What a glorious company they were those heroes and heroines of the Bible whose deeds were recorded but whose names were not given!

There is another book kept by the One who never slumbers nor forgets, and in that book the anonymous great have their names as well as their deeds recorded. After all, a deed without a name is better than a name without a deed.

PLAIN SPEECH is to be admired, but a lot that passes for plain is simply rude. The trouble with the man who boasts that he calls a spade a spade is that he often ends by calling everything a spade. He sneers at every tender emotion, brands with the name of spade every simple human joy and is buried at last with a spade, the latter office being perhaps the kindest one that humble implement ever performed for him. May God keep fresh the fountain of our laughter and our tears!

I N BASEBALL a player always goes back and sits down after he strikes out. It would help matters in many a church if that rule could be applied to board members.

A NOTHER FELLOW out our way gets a little cheap patronizing notice in the newspapers by winning a Bible-reading marathon. Not Bible reading but Bible obeying counts with God. And the winners will not be known till we all stand before the judgment seat of Christ.

P EOPLE, NOT ideas, should get first attention from the preacher. Yet we find many talented men who are cold toward people but fervent in their love for ideas. Terrible as it may be, it is yet true that one may spend a lifetime propagating religious ideas with little or no love for men back of it all.

I T IS not a sign of health when a Christian begins to apologize for being human. Our Lord's incarnation proved forever the intrinsic excellence of human nature apart from sin. The ages have shown the folly of trying to escape from our humanity. The monks tried to be less than human, the mystics to be more than human, but nature caught up with both of them at last.

To my mind the most ominous sign of the times is the secularization of religion. When Rome began to laugh at her gods, her end was in sight.

Today a barely secularized Christianity has become popular in literature and on the stage. The appearance of so many shows with the religious motif may look encouraging, but actually they have worked to destroy what remained of reverence for holy things, and the result is that men have no longer any sanctuaries.

"The Green Pastures," a show so widely praised a few years ago and still popular, is probably the top flight in things sacrilegious. The heart shudders at the thought of "De Lawd" smoking a black cigar and talking in the coarse language of a Harlem nightclub.

America should take warning. When there is nothing left that is sacred, there is nothing left that is safe.

It is amazing the distance some Christians go to seek persecution and all so unnecessary. Draw a little nearer to Calvary, and persecution will seek you. The world still hates the man who hates his sin.

DAVID

He tore from his own heart
The sounding strings,
And builded
In the window
Of the Synagogue and Church
A thousand harps,
To turn the winds of fury into song.

A FALSE TEST for religion is the so-called practi-
cal one: If it alleviates human suffering and
makes its possessor live a better life, it is of God.
That does not by any means follow. True salvation must provide deliverance from death and protection from the wrath of a justly angry God. Any
preachment that overlooks these important things
is dealing only with surface problems. Death is
worse than disease and hell is worse than poverty.
Every social reformer must meet this test or be rejected.

In the Voice of A.W. Tozer: